Basic for Islam

An Ideal Gift for the Young Brother of the Ummah

Tuhfatush Shabaab

Published by:

Islamic Book Store
302 Saad Residancy
Shahin Park M G Road
Bardoli Surat India
394601
Ph. 0091 9979353876

Contents

Introduction i

Part 1 1

   Chapter 1 2

      BULOOGH (PUBERTY) 2

      CLEANLINESS 3

      ISTINJAA 4

      CIRCUMCISION 6

      JANAABAT & WETDREAMS 8

   Chapter 2 10

      HAIR 10

      CLOTHES 16

      PERFUME (ITAR) 23

   Chapter 3 27

      PHYSICAL FITNESS - TRAINING 27

      PERMISSIBLE SPORTS 27

   Chapter 4 – Bad Habits 36

      MUSIC 36

      SMOKING 38

INTOXICANTS 42

GAMBLING 45

Part 2 50

Chapter 5 51

Harms of Casting Lustful Glances 51

PHOTOGRAPHY, VIDEOS, TELEVISION, CELL PHONES, D.V.D, YOU TUBE, ETC 58

PORNOGRAPHY 59

MASTURBATION 67

ZINA / FORNICATION / ADULTERY 69

MARRIAGE 71

SUICIDE 72

Chapter 6 77

CONDUCT AT HOME 77

DUTY AT HOME 78

MASHWARA (Consulting) 79

ALWAYS HAVE A GOAL 79

NEVER BE IDLE 80

EMPLOYMENT 81

7 HABITS OF A SUCCESSFUL MUSLIM YOUTH 82

Conclusion 87

Notes 92

Introduction

Allah Ta'ala has created the human being as 'ASHRAFUL MAKHLOOQAAT' (the best of His creation). In order to guide His creation, He sent many messengers and revealed Divine Books.

The change from childhood to adulthood for a Muslim begins with Buloogh (puberty). Apart from physical changes (which take place inside our bodies), we undergo emotional changes (the way we feel), as well as mental changes (the way we understand things). It is, therefore, very important for us to understand and prepare for this transformation and change.

This transition to adulthood comes with huge responsibilities. This body is an amaanah (trust) from Allah Ta'ala. We use it to make the ibaadah (worship) of Allah Ta'ala. Therefore, it is important that we take care of it as best we can in order to fulfil the rights of Allah Ta'ala and protect ourselves from Nafs (the carnal desires) and Shaytaan.

In Arabic there is a saying, "Youth is a kind of Madness." This statement shows the delicate nature of the youth. They can be swayed in any direction depending on the environment and company they keep. Many challenges and evil influences are gripping the youth of today. It is important that we provide them with guidance to protect themselves from these evils.

This book was compiled to help the youth identify these evils and dissuade them from it. It also provides them with some solutions if they have succumbed to these influences. It is the responsibility of the teachers to expand on the topics provided in the book and give them detailed explanations and answer their questions. **Some sections are of a sensitive nature and should not be discussed in the presence of young children.**

The contents have been extracted from different books and articles which are relevant to the topics discussed. We acknowledge and are obliged to all the authors of these books and articles for their research etc.

We express our gratitude to our creator Allah Ta'ala and to all those who contributed to this book in compiling and editing this book. We humbly request you to make dua for all those contributed to this book in any way whatsoever. May Allah reward them and their families with His pleasure, grant them sincerity, forgiveness, true success in this world and the Akhirah and use them for the effort of his Deen. Aameen!

Rabbana taqabal minna Innaka Antas Sameeul Aleem wa tub Alayna innaka antat Tawaaabur Rahim

We ask Allah Ta'ala to accept our feeble efforts, for verily He is all hearing and all-knowing and we beseech His forgiveness as He is most forgiving and merciful. Aameen

This book is a **"Gift for the Youth"** and is therefore dedicated to them. May it be a means of guidance and help for them in this most challenging time of their life. *Aameen.*

We humbly ask the readers to notify the Publishers of any errors and inaccuracies as this is the first edition of the book. Your input will be greatly appreciated and will be considered in future editions insha Allah.

Ta'limi Board (KZN)

April 2016

Part 1

In this section ... ...

- Buloogh (Puberty)
- Cleanliness, Istinjaa, Circumcision, Janaabat, etc.
- Hair, Clothing, Perfume
- Physical Fitness, Permissible Sport
- Music, Smoking, Intoxicant, Gambling

Chapter 1

BULOOGH (PUBERTY)

The body of a male undergoes many changes from the age of eleven to fifteen. This is a sign that he is now reaching **PUBERTY**. Once a boy reaches the age of puberty, all the laws of Shariah become fardh (compulsory) upon him.

WHAT ARE THE SIGNS OF PUBERTY?

Puberty is when many changes take place in a person's body as he becomes a man. Some of the signs are:

1. A boy may start gaining weight and his muscles develop. His shoulders and chest broaden and he may grow taller in a short space of time.
2. Hair growth increases over other areas of his body. A thicker, darker growth of hair will be found on his legs, feet, arms, underarms, face and pubic area (private parts).
3. His voice may 'break or crack'.
4. He may experience pain in his legs as his bones begin growing at a faster rate and his muscles become stretched.
5. He may experience a wet dream when semen comes out of his front private part. An erection is also normal.

Change is unique to each individual. A boy should not compare himself to others.

Accept these changes, as your journey to manhood is now beginning.

CLEANLINESS

Cleanliness is Half of Imaan (faith).

As we grow older, we should become more conscious of our personal hygiene. It is important that we always remain pure and clean.

1. During the summer months, we should bath more regularly as we tend to perspire more in the heat.
2. Apply Itar (perfume) as it is sunnah to do so.
3. We should be particular about clipping our nails every week (preferably on a Thursday night or Friday) and keeping our hair short, neat and of one length.
4. Shave the hair under the arms and around the private areas once a week or at least once every two weeks. A razor or shaving cream may be used. Remember, we cannot allow this hair to grow for more than forty days as it is a MAJOR SIN to do so.
5. Clothes should be changed regularly.
6. Make a habit of remaining in wudhu. There are many benefits of staying in the state of wudhu. Wudhu keeps a person refreshed. Those parts that are washed during wudhu will shine on the day of Qiyaamah.

Chapter 1

ISTINJAA

WHAT IS ISTINJAA?

Istinjaa is to clean the private parts with water after relieving oneself.

There are many etiquettes to follow regarding istinjaa:

1. It is not permissible to expose one's satr in the presence of people while relieving or cleansing oneself. (Satr: From the navel to below the knees). We should be particularly mindful of this when using public toilets, school change rooms, gyms, swimming pools, beaches etc.
2. One should avoid spending unnecessary time in the toilet.
3. There should be no talking, whistling or singing whilst relieving oneself.
4. It is makrooh tahrimi to face the Qiblah or have the back facing the Qiblah whilst relieving oneself.
5. One should refrain from reading books, newspapers or playing with the cell phone in the toilet.
6. Make istinjaa with the left hand.
7. After relieving oneself, wait till all the drops of urine have left the private part. This is called ISTIBRAA. One may cough to ensure that every drop of urine has left the system.
8. Another way of making Istibraa is to place toilet paper on your private part and take several steps whereby the urine drops leak out onto the toilet paper.
9. As an extra precautionary method, one can place a piece of toilet paper in his underpants to absorb any leftover droplets of urine. One should only commence performing *Wudhu* after

feeling assured that no more drops of urine will come out. Before performing *Salaah*, the toilet paper should be removed.

URINATING WHILE STANDING

1. It is not permissible to stand and urinate.
2. There is a great danger of urine messing the clothes, body and the toilet.
3. Istinjaa and cleansing is difficult in such a posture.
4. It's against the Sunnah to do so.
5. Always use a low pan when relieving oneself as it is a sunnah of Rasulullah ﷺ to relieve oneself in this manner. It is also more healthy and easier to clean oneself. It also prevents our clothes and body from becoming messed by the unclean water of the toilet bowl in a high pan toilet.
6. It is sunnah to sit in a squatting posture when relieving oneself. It has many medical benefits and prevents one from many sicknesses.
7. Remember, when using the low pan toilet, lower your pants till above your knee not till the ankles otherwise your pants will become soiled.
8. If you don't know how to use the low pan toilet, ask someone elder to teach you how to use it. Make intention that if you build a home one day, you will have the Sunnah low pan toilet.

Chapter 1

CIRCUMCISION

WHAT IS CIRCUMCISION?

Circumcision means to remove the foreskin at the front end of the penis.

1. Circumcision was the Sunnah of all the Ambiyaa.
2. Circumcision is amongst the distinguishing traits of a Muslim.
3. Circumcision should be done as soon as possible after birth or after accepting Islam.

THE BENEFITS OF CIRCUMCISION

1. It ensures perfect cleanliness since the drops of urine are not held back by the foreskin.
2. It is conducive to good health, cleanliness and prevents many sicknesses.
3. It decreases sensual desires.
4. It prevents many diseases.
5. It is a Sunnah practice.
6. Above all, it is the command of Allah Ta'ala and OUR SUBMISSION TO THE COMMAND OF ALLAH Ta'ala SHOULD BE regarded as the greatest benefit.

NB. Circumcision is not a pre-requisite for becoming a Muslim. The earlier it is done the better. However, one may delay it for a suitable time like the holidays or long weekends etc., allowing time for recovery. Nowadays circumcision has become very easy and pain free.

Questions

1. What is puberty?

2. List three signs of puberty?

3. How should one keep the body pure and fresh at all times?

4. How often should unwanted hair be removed?

5. What is the method of making Istinjaa?

6. Which areas of the body are prohibited for males to expose?

7. Is it permissible to stand and urinate?

8. What are the benefits of circumcision? _____
_____
_____

9. Circumcision is the command of _____ and the sunnah of all the _____.

JANAABAT & WETDREAMS

WHAT IS JANAABAT?

Janaabat is a state of impurity which makes ghusal compulsory. If a person discharges semen, in his sleep or when awake, he gets into a state of Janaabat and ghusal becomes fardh upon him.

WHAT IS A WET DREAM?

1. When sperm is released from ones front private part whilst one is asleep. It may be because of a dream of a sexual nature, because of which one ejaculates (releases semen).
2. A wet dream generally marks the start of buloogh (puberty).
3. Wet dreams are at time, the result of the influences of the shayaateen.
4. Some remember their wet dreams and others don't. In all cases, as long as one notices semen on one's body or clothing, it becomes compulsory to have ghusl and to remove the traces of semen from the body and clothing.

5. Some common signs of ejaculation are: a) weakness. b) wetness on one's body or clothes.
6. Other causes for wet dreams are: a) not protecting the eyes from evil. b) Eating too rich or spicy foods. c) Being affected by shaytaan.
7. It is important that one visits the toilet and passes urine before ghusl so that no semen remains in the system.
8. Once in the state of janaabat, one should not delay in performing ghusl.
9. Semen is impure. If it falls onto one's clothing, body, or bedding one should ensure that it is washed off thoroughly to make it pure.

WHAT IS PROHIBITED IN SUCH A STATE?

1. Performing Salaah.
2. Tawaaf of the Ka'aba.
3. Entering the masjid.
4. Touching or reciting the Qur-aan.
5. It is makrooh to remove any unwanted hair during the state of Janaabat.

Note: Rinse your clothing before putting it into the laundry.

Chapter 2

HAIR

The hair that grows on the head of a person is a great favour of Allah Ta'ala. It increases the beauty of a person. Nabi ﷺ has said, "Anyone who has hair, then let him honour it." (Abu Dawood)

We should appreciate this bounty of Allah Ta'ala by following these etiquettes:

1. One should keep one's hair neat. Nabi ﷺ disliked one's hair to be untidy.
2. A man should cut his hair evenly on his head.
3. It is forbidden to grow part of the hair and shave part of the hair on the head. This prohibition includes hairstyles such as: wedge, mushroom, spikes and many other weird modern day hairstyles that are against the Shariah.
4. The maximum length a male is allowed to keep his hair is up to the shoulder. This is in accordance to Sunnah and is called "Zulfaa".
5. Men are not allowed to resemble women in the way they keep their hair. Therefore one cannot keep the hair longer than the shoulder, plaited or in a ponytail.
6. Rasulullah ﷺ always began with the right when combing the hair.

7. It is preferable to part the hair in the middle and not to have a fixed habit of choosing the right or left side.
8. Men are not allowed to wear wigs or hairpieces whether natural or artificial.
9. Hair implantation is also not allowed.
10. One should not apply gel to the hair. Many gels are such that it prevents water from reaching the hair or scalp; as a result one's wudhu is left incomplete.
11. It is Sunnah to oil the hair of the head especially on a Friday.

NB. Those who are obsessed with hairstyles generally don't like wearing a topee (hat) or turban. This is a sign of such people suffering from an inferiority complex with regard to their identity and Deen. May Allah Ta'ala save us. Aameen.

THE BEARD

Rasulullah ﷺ instructed the trimming of the moustache and ordered the lengthening of the beard. The beard is a salient feature of Islam and is the distinguishing feature between a male and female. A Muslim who does not keep a beard is breaking an important law of Islam. It is WAAJIB (necessary) for males to keep a beard.

WHAT IS THE SIGNIFICANCE OF THE BEARD?

1. It was a practice of Rasulullah ﷺ and all the Prophets (alayhimus salaam) before him.
2. The beard is a sign of a Muslim, while to shave the beard is the way of the Kuffaar.
3. It differentiates between a male and female.
4. The beard has always been the sign of piety and respect of a man.

Chapter 2

HOW DOES ONE MAINTAIN A BEARD?

1. Grow the beard until it is one fist in length.
2. When it grows beyond one fist in length, trim it up to one fist so that it remains neat.
3. It is Sunnah to oil and comb the beard.
4. It is Sunnah to apply itar to ones beard.
5. To grow the moustache such that it covers the upper lip is makrooh. One should keep the moustache short and neat.

CAUTION AGAINST NOT KEEPING A BEARD

1. The nation of Hadhrat Lut (alayhis salaam) was destroyed due to ten crimes, one of which was trimming and shaving the beard.
2. It is not permissible to keep a short beard (less than a fist in length) and regard this as a legitimate beard. However, if naturally ones beard doesn't grow longer than this then there is no sin.
3. A person is not sinful if his beard naturally does not grow. If only a few strands of hair grows, he should not pluck or shave it off.
4. The hair that grows below the lower lip is part of the beard and is called the baby beard. It is not permissible to shave that hair.
5. The beard is the hair that grows along the jaw bone from the middle of one ear to the other ear and as well as the hair below the lower lip.

Once, a person with dishevelled hair and an untidy beard walked into Masjidun Nabawi. Nabi ﷺ indicated to him to neaten his hair and trim his beard (that exceeded one fist). A few moments later he returned with neat and tidy hair. Nabi ﷺ said, "Is it not better to have ones hair neat and well arranged, instead of walking about with dishevelled hair, like shaytaan?"(Mishkaat)

CUTTING AND DISPOSING OF HAIR AND NAILS

1. It is permissible to cut the hair and nails on any day of the week.
2. It is permissible to clip ones nails at night.
3. According to a Hadith it is good for the health to cut one's nails on a Thursday after Maghrib or on a Friday. (Mirqaat)
4. It is makrooh to cut ones hair or trim ones nails in the state of janaabat.
5. Removed hair and nails should not be thrown into a bin; instead it should be buried or thrown into a river (after reciting Bismillah).
6. The mustahab method of removing hair from the armpit is to commence with the hair on the right armpit and then the left armpit. One may shave or pluck the hair under the arms.
7. It is permissible to pluck out strands of hair that emerge from the nose and ears.
8. Rasulullah ﷺ has cursed those who shape their eyebrows. (Mirqaat).
9. The mustahab method of cutting one's nails is to begin with the shahaadah finger of the right hand up to the baby finger of the right hand. Thereafter, continue with the baby finger of the left hand up to the thumb of the left hand. Lastly, cut the nail of the thumb of the right hand.

TIME LIMITS

1. One must clip his nails and trim his moustache once a week.

Chapter 2

2. Remove the hair of the pubic areas and the armpits every week, two weeks or three weeks.
3. If the hair is not shaved or the nails are not clipped for more than forty days, a person will be committing a major sin. However, his Salaah and other ibaadaat will be valid.

GREY HAIR

1. According to a Hadith, "Grey hair is the noor of a Mu'min. When a man goes grey, then for every grey hair is recorded a virtuous deed and for each hair he is elevated in rank."(Mishkaat)
2. It is not permissible to dye the hair black pretending to be young.
3. It is makrooh to pluck or cut only the white hair from the beard or head.
4. It is Sunnah to apply mehndi to the hair of the head and beard. (Sublime conduct)

QUESTIONS

1. What is janaabat? _____

2. Is it permissible for a person to have intercourse outside marriage?

3. What is a wet dream? How should you purify yourself after having a wet dream?

4. List four things that are not permissible to do during the state of janaabat?

5. What types of haircuts are not accepted in Islam?

6. What is the minimum length a beard can be shortened to?

7. Mention the Hadith where Nabi ﷺ prohibited a Sahaabah from shortening the beard and lengthening the moustache?

Chapter 2

8. List 5 points on how one should cut his hair and nails and how to dispose of it.

9. What is the rule on dyeing ones hair black?

10. Is it permissible to pluck/cut white hair from the head and beard?

CLOTHES

A human being is born with several basic needs. One of them is the need for clothing. To cover one's body is not just a need but part of human nature. In addition to being a natural need, the Shariah has commanded us to cover our bodies. The following are certain guidelines in this regard:

THE KURTA

1. Nabi ﷺ has preferred the kurta over all other types of clothing. (Tirmizi)
2. The Kurta is the best way of covering ones satr in a modest manner.
3. The Kurta of Nabi ﷺ would reach around the middle of his calves (above his ankles), while the sleeves would reach up to the wrist.

CLOTHING ABOVE THE ANKLES

1. Rasulullah ﷺ has said: "Whatever clothing flows below the ankles will be in the fire."(Bukhaari)
2. Another Hadith states: "Allah Ta'ala will NOT look at the person with mercy who out of pride allows his clothes to flow (beneath the ankles)." (Abu Dawood)

Note: Wearing our clothes below the ankles is a sign of pride. Why should we resemble the proud ones?

WEARING CLOTHING TO BOAST

Hadith: Whoever wears clothing to show off and to attract attention will be made to wear the same clothing in the Hereafter, before being flung with it into the fire. (Abu Dawood)

WHAT IS BOASTFUL CLOTHING?

Such clothing that a person wears so that he may become the centre of attraction and people will praise him.

Chapter 2

WHAT TYPE OF CLOTHING SHOULD ONE WEAR?

1. One should wear simple clothes which is neat, conceals the body and is according to the commands of Allah Ta'ala.
2. One can wear beautiful clothing, with the intention that Allah Ta'ala is beautiful and loves beautiful things.
3. One can wear beautiful clothing to show gratitude to Allah Ta'ala for the bounties He has bestowed on us.
4. The best and most beautiful clothing to wear are those which Nabi ﷺ, the Sahaabah (radiyallahu anhum) and the pious Ulama wear.
5. One should wear his best and most beautiful clothing on Fridays and on the days of Eid.

WARNING TO MEN AND WOMEN WHO IMITATE ONE ANOTHER IN DRESSING

1. HADITH: Nabi ﷺ has cursed those men who imitate women and those women who imitate men. (Bukhari)
2. Sayyiduna Abu Umaamah (radiyallahu anhu) narrates: Four types of people are cursed in this world and in the Aakhirah, and the angels say *Aameen* to those curses. One of them is a person whom Allah Ta'ala has created as a man but he behaves like a woman. (Targhib Vol 3)
3. Men are not permitted to wear bangles, rubber bands, ear rings, studs, rings, chains, etc. Due to the above Hadith, males must also avoid putting mehndi on their hands and fingernails.
4. Men are forbidden from wearing gold rings. It is permissible for the Qadhi or the leader of the Muslims to wear a silver ring.
5. The fashion of males piercing their ears is also included in imitating a female and is not permissible.

WEARING UN-ISLAMIC CLOTHING

1. Muslims have their own identity and clothing.
2. Nabi ﷺ said: "Whoever imitates a nation will be regarded as one of them." (Abu Dawood)
3. Hadhrat Abdullah ibn Amar ibnul-Aas (radiyallahu anhu) narrates that one day Nabi ﷺ saw him wearing yellow clothing. Nabi ﷺ said: "Remove this clothing as it is the colour of the disbelievers." He asked Nabi ﷺ, "Should I wash it (the colour away)". Nabi ﷺ said, "No! Burn it!" (Muslim)
4. Abdullah ibn Umar (radiyallahu anhu) narrates that Nabi ﷺ saw him wearing red clothing and said to him, "This is the [colour of the] garments of the disbelievers. Do not wear it!" (Muslim Vol 2)
5. Males are prohibited from wearing silk clothing.
6. It is not permissible to use any item or clothing that has animate pictures on it.
7. It is not permissible to wear a tie as it is a resemblance of the christian cross.
8. Men should avoid wearing clothing or shoes which resemble that of females, e.g. pink, orange and red kurtas/shirts or trousers and other bright and gaudy colours.
9. Do not become walking billboards by wearing T-Shirts or jackets that promote and advertise certain products or sports etc.

ALTERING ONES APPEARANCE UNNATURALLY

1. It is haraam to alter our bodies which Allah Ta'ala has given us. People who thin their teeth or tattoo their bodies or seek

beauty by resorting to plastic surgery are cursed by Allah Ta'ala.

2. In Surah Nisaa, Allah Ta'ala says, "Shaytaan said, 'I will mislead them and I will create in them false desires; I will order them to slit the ear of the cattle and to deface features and attributes created by Allah.'" This shows us the plan of shaytaan. He deceptively misleads us into doubting the way we look and plays with our doubts and self-esteem.

3. We need to be constantly strengthening our Imaan and building our defence against shaytaani traps.

4. Hadhrat Umar (radiyallah anhu) narrates that Nabi ﷺ said, "Allah Ta'ala curses the woman who adorns the hair of others (by means of hair extensions) and the one who desires such adornment of hair, those who tattoo others and who are tattooed." (Bukhaari)

5. We should be grateful for the body Allah Ta'ala has blessed us with. We should not suffer from an inferiority complex (which could lead to ingratitude).

6. That part of the body which is tattooed will be punished in Jahannam.

7. We should even avoid fake tattoos as it prevents water from reaching the skin during wudhu and ghusl.

BODY PIERCINGS

1. Rasulullah ﷺ has said: "He who imitates a nation is counted to be from amongst them."

2. On many occasions, Rasulullah ﷺ has prohibited us from imitating the ways of the enemies of Allah Ta'ala and to be unique in our ways of life by distinguishing ourselves from their weird ways.

3. The piercing of the navel, tongue, eyebrows, etc. is an act that has been initiated by the Kuffaar as a fashion craze; and it is a salient feature of the open sinners.
4. Another reason for impermissibility is that by piercing these body parts one would unnecessarily be undergoing discomfort and pain. Shariah does not permit one to subject the body to unnecessary pain. Therefore one should abstain from these practices.
5. The body is an Amaanat (trust) from Allah Ta'ala and we will be questioned regarding it.

THE TOPEE

Wearing a topee is a sign of a Muslim. Muslims around the world wear topees as this is a symbol of Islam and distinguishes a Muslim. Rasulullah ﷺ and all the Sahaabah used to wear topees.

1. To be bareheaded without a valid reason is makrooh.
2. Hadhrat Abdullah ibn Umar (radiyallahu anhu) narrates that Rasulullah ﷺ used to wear a round white topee. (Tabrani)
3. Ibnul Arabi (rahimahullah) writes: The topee is amongst the clothing of the Ambiyaa (alayhimus salaam) and the pious ones. It protects the head and keeps the turban in place which is sunnah.
4. Nabi ﷺ was never seen without a topee except while he was in ihraam.

Chapter 2

THE TURBAN (AMAAMAH)

1. Nabi ﷺ said: "Wear the turban as it is a sign of Islam and it distinguishes between a Muslim and a Kaafir". (Khasaaile Nabawi Pg. 6)
2. The Sahaabah (radiyallahu anhum) and scholars of Hadith were also steadfast on tying the amaamah.

VIRTUES OF A TURBAN

1. Nabi ﷺ said: "Allah causes His mercy to descend on the people wearing turbans on the day of Jumuah and His angels make dua for such people. (Majma)
2. The angels attend the Jumu'ah while wearing turbans. Hence, those people who are wearing turbans receive the benefit that the angels make dua for them till sunset. (Dailami)
3. The Fuqahaa (jurist) have accepted the fact that Salaah performed while wearing a turban is greater in reward than one performed without it.

IMPORTANT TO CONSIDER

When a person performs Salaah, he should understand that he is standing in the presence of Allah Ta'ala. Therefore, he should dress respectfully. It is haraam to dress in the evil styles of the Kuffaar when standing in Allah's presence.

It is very disrespectful to enter a masjid with T-shirts and other types of clothing on which slogans, logos and inscriptions appear, even if the pictures are of inanimate objects.

We should remember well, that we are always ambassadors of Islam and we should not have an inferiority complex about the difference in our dress compared to the current trends.

A Muslim does not follow trends and is not dictated by changing conditions. Rather a Muslim influences conditions around him.

PERFUME (ITAR)

Nabi ﷺ was very fond of itar and never refused a gift of itar. Nabi ﷺ said that musk is the best perfume. (Nasai)

One should apply itar on the following occasions:

1. The day of Jumuah.
2. The day of Eid.
3. When acquiring the knowledge of Islam.
4. When attending Islamic functions and gatherings.
5. Before entering the state of ihram.
6. Before meeting your wife.

Please take note of the following:

1. Avoid using such a strong chemical itar that causes headaches and skin rashes, etc.
2. Don't force anyone to apply itar. Many people are sensitive to strong smells and may not be comfortable using your brand of itr. Offer them and if they refuse don't feel offended.

Chapter 2

QUESTIONS

1. Which way of dressing was preferred by Nabi ﷺ?

2. Mention the two Ahaadith warning us against keeping the trousers below the ankles?

3. What clothes are regarded as boastful clothing?

4. What are the effects of wearing branded clothing?

5. With what intention should one wear beautiful clothes?

6. What type of clothing is preferred for a Muslim?

7. Describe one of the four types of people who are cursed in this world and the next? _____
_____
_____
_____

8. List five ways that men imitate woman? _____
_____
_____
_____

9. Why is putting tattoos, doing plastic surgery or shaping ones eyebrows not allowed in Islam? _____
_____
_____

10. Why are fake tattoos not allowed in Islam? _____
_____
_____

11. Why did Nabi ﷺ prohibit us from imitating the ways of the enemies of Islam? _____

Chapter 2

12. Why are piercings of the tongue, eyebrows and navel etc. not allowed in Islam?

13. Why is being bareheaded for no reason not allowed in Islam?

14. Nabi ﷺ was never seen without a topi except when Nabi ﷺ was in _____ .

15. What did Nabi ﷺ say regarding a turban?

16. What did Nabi ﷺ say regarding a person who wears turban on a Friday?

17. On which occasions should one apply itr?

Chapter 3

PHYSICAL FITNESS - TRAINING

Hadith: Rasulullah ﷺ said "A strong believer is better than a weak believer."

Islam teaches us to keep healthy and fit. The time of puberty is a good time to pay attention to one's health and physique. Islam lays stress on physical training and exercises which help to protect oneself and society. One should bear in mind that physical training and methods of defence should be practiced within the laws of Shariah.

PERMISSIBLE SPORTS

SELF DEFENCE

Self-defence is permissible and encouraged in Islam. Extra caution must be taken whilst practicing that the head and face are not aimed at.

One should not conduct oneself aggressively or use this skill offensively or to oppress anybody. It is not permissible to bow the head, as is common at the beginning of any karate session.

Chapter 3

ARCHERY

Nabi ﷺ encouraged archery. It is reported in a Hadith: "Practice shooting arrows and horse riding." (Mishkaat)

Nabi ﷺ has mentioned many virtues regarding archery and declared learning it as a means of attaining reward from Allah Ta'ala. Archery creates liveliness and alertness in the body, strengthens the muscles and enhances the eyesight.

An amazing incident of a brave young Sahaabi

Ghabah was a small village about four or five miles from Madinah Munawwarah. Nabi's ﷺ camels were sent to that place for grazing. Abdur Rahmaan Fazari, with the help of a few disbelievers, killed the person looking after the camels and stole them. The thieves were riding horses and all of them were armed. Salamah bin Akwah (radiyallahu anhu) was going on foot in the morning with his bow and arrows when he saw the thieves. Although he was only a boy, he ran very fast. It is said that he could beat the fastest horse in a race. He was also a very good archer (expert shooter with the bow and arrow).

As soon as he saw the thieves he climbed up a hill and shouted towards Madinah Munawwarah to call for help. He then chased the thieves and on approaching them, started shooting arrows one after the other. He did this so quickly and continuously that the thieves thought they were being chased by a large number of people. If any of the thieves happened to turn his horse towards him, he hid behind a tree and shot the animal with his arrows. The thieves ran off at full speed fearing that they would be caught.

Salamah (radiyallahu anhu) says: "I kept on chasing them until all the camels taken away by them were behind me. While escaping they left behind 30 spears and 30 sheets of cloth of their own. Meanwhile, Uyaynah bin Hisn (another thief) and his party arrived to help the thieves. They had meanwhile come to know that I was all alone. They now chased me in large numbers and I was forced to climb up a hill. As they were about to approach me, I shouted, 'Stop. First listen to me. Do you know who am I? I am Ibnul Akwah. By Him who has given glory to Muhammad ﷺ, if anyone of you chases me, he cannot catch me. On the other hand, if I run after any of you he cannot escape me.' I kept on talking to them in this manner to delay them till, I thought, help would reach me from Madinah Munawwarah. I looked anxiously through the trees, as I talked to them when at last; I noticed a group of riders headed by Akhram Asadi (radiyallahu anhu) coming towards me. As Akhram (radiyallahu anhu) approached the bandits, he attacked Abdur Rahman and cut one leg of his horse. As Abdur Rahmaan fell down from his horse, he attacked Akhram and killed him. Abu Qataadah (radiyallahu anhu) had meanwhile arrived. In the fighting that took place Abdur Rahmaan lost his life and Abu Qataadah (radiyallahu anhu) lost his horse."

It is written in some books of history that, when Akhram was going to attack Abdur Rahmaan, Salamah (radiyallahu anhu) advised him to wait till the rest of his people had joined him but he did not wait, saying: "I wish to die in the path of Allah."

He was the only person killed from among the Muslims. The bandits lost a good number of their men. More help reached the Muslims and the thieves ran away. Salamah (radiyallahu anhu) asked for Nabi's ﷺ permission to chase them saying: "O, Nabi of Allah! Let me have one hundred men, I shall teach them a lesson."

Nabi ﷺ said: "No. They would have reached their homes by now."

Most of the historians say that Salamah (radiyallahu anhu) was about 12 or 13 years old at that time. Look, how a boy of such a small age was able to chase so many bandits single-handed. He recovered all the stolen goods and also took a great amount of booty from them. This was the result of Imaan and Ikhlaas, courage and strength which Allah Ta'ala had filled in the hearts of those blessed people.

HORSE RIDING

Horse riding is very beneficial as it provides good exercise to the body; it develops qualities such as skill, bravery, courage and high ambitions within a person.

Nabi ﷺ said, "Whoever rears a horse to use it in the path of Allah with full expectation of reward, then all the fodder and water the horse will fill its stomach with and even the droppings and urine will be weighed (along with his other good deeds) on the day of Qiyaamah." (Bukhaari)

WRESTLING

Nabi ﷺ wrestled with Sayyiduna Rukaanah [radiyallahu anhu] (a skilled and highly regarded wrestler) and beat him.

NB: The sensational wrestling that the entertainment industry presents is not the pure art of wrestling which is mentioned here.

A wrestling contest between two young Sahaabah

During the time of Rasulullah ﷺ, whenever an army of Muslims moved out from Madinah Munawwarah for battle, Nabi ﷺ inspected them at some distance outside the town. It was here that he usually returned all those boys to Madinah Munawwarah, who were too young to fight, but in their eagerness had joined the army.

After setting out for Uhud, Nabi ﷺ carried out an inspection just outside Madinah Munawwarah. He ordered the young boys to go back.

Among them were Abdullah bin Umar, Zaid bin Saabit, Usamah bin Zaid, Zaid bin Arqam, Bara bin Aazib, Amr bin Hazam, Usaid bin Zubair, 'Urabah bin Aus, Abu Sa'eed Khudri, Samurah bin Jundub and Raafi' bin Khudaij (radiyallhu anhum). All of them had just entered their teens.

Raafi' bin Khudaij (radiyallahu anhu) said to Nabi ﷺ: "O Nabi of Allah! My son Raafi' is a very good archer."

Hadhrat Raafi' (radiyallahu anhu) stood on his toes to show himself to be taller than he actually was. Nabi ﷺ permitted him to stay on. When Samurah bin Jundub (radiyallahu anhu) learnt about this, he complained to his stepfather Murrah bin Sanan saying: "Nabi ﷺ has allowed Raafi' and rejected me. I am sure to beat him in a wrestling contest and therefore, I am more deserving of Nabi's ﷺ favour."

This was reported to Nabi ﷺ who allowed Samurah to prove his claim by wrestling with Raafi'. Samurah actually beat Raafi' in the fight and he too was permitted to join the army. A few more boys made similar efforts to stay on and some of them were given permission.

HUNTING

It is lawful to hunt animals which are permissible to consume. It is not permissible to hunt purely for the sake of sport or enjoyment. This is due to the fact that the animal is distressed, injured or killed just for our entertainment. This is a form of oppression for which a person will be taken into account on the day of Qiyaamah. This law applies for anything which has life including fish. Therefore sport-fishing and the use of live bait is impermissible. The purpose of hunting must be to eat the meat of the animal.

Chapter 3

SWIMMING

There is a narration which says: "The best activity for the believer is swimming and the best activity for women is knitting."

Another narration states: Anything which is not included in the remembrance of Allah Ta'ala is *Lahw* and *La'ib* (useless and futile) except for four things; playing with one's wife, training one's horses, walking between two targets (while aiming arrows i.e. practicing archery) and (learning and) teaching how to swim.

Swimming is an excellent means of physical exercise. It strengthens the body muscles and keeps the body strong and healthy.

KEEP THE FOLLOWING POINTS IN MIND

1. Clothing for exercise must cover the body from the navel to below the knee and must be loose and not tight fitting.
2. Select an appropriate place. It must not be a place that where males and females mingle freely or where music is blaring etc.
3. Do not devote yourself to exercise at the expense of your other duties towards Allah Ta'ala or towards other people.

THE SHAR-EE VIEW REGARDING PRESENT DAY SPORTS

It should be borne in mind that spectating of sports has many evils due to which it is not permissible.

Firstly, people mostly view sports on television, which is prohibited. Television condones photography of animate objects, cameras focus on the satr (private areas) of participants and females in the audience. Even if a sport is viewed live, there are many evils involved. Included are, looking at the satr of males or females, intermingling, becoming negligent of

Salaah, the love for sport stars enter our hearts and we begin to praise the players.

Praising an open sinner invites the anger of Allah Ta'ala and causes the Arsh of Allah Ta'ala to shake. The spectating of sports falls under the law of lahw (that which is useless and non-beneficial), due to it being a waste of valuable time. Just this law alone is sufficient to render spectating of sports as unlawful.

Many a time fights and arguments break out as a result of one team losing a match. Sometimes families break up ties and stop speaking with each another over disputes relating to sports.

Gambling is also a major factor in many sports. Millions of dollars are wasted daily as a result of games and sports.

In the light of the above it is very clear that wasting ones time viewing and following sports is totally impermissible.

An amazing incident of the bravery of two young Sahaabah

Hadhrat Abdur Rahman bin 'Auf (radiyallahu anhu), one of the most famous Sahaabah, narrates: "In the battle of Badr, I was standing in the fighting line when I noticed two Ansaar youngsters, one on either side. I thought it would have been better if I had been between strong men who could help me in need. Suddenly one of the boys caught my hand and said, 'Uncle, do you know Abu Jahl?' I said, 'Yes, but what do you mean by this?' He said, 'I have come to know that the terrible man speaks bad things about Nabi ﷺ. By Him who holds my life in His hand, if I see him, I will not leave him until I kill him or I am killed.' His words left me wonderstruck. Then the other boy had a similar talk with me. I happened to notice Abu Jahl running about in the battlefield on the back of his horse. I said to the boys, 'There is Abu Jahl.' Both of them immediately rushed towards him and started attacking him with their swords, until I saw him fall from the back of his horse."

These boys were Hadhrat Mu'aaz bin Amr bin Jamooh (radiyallahu anhu) and Mu'aaz bin Afra (radiyallahu anhu).

Mu'aaz bin Amr bin Jamooh (radiyallahu anhu) says: "I had heard the people say, 'No one can kill Abu Jahl. He is very well guarded'. At that time, I had promised to finish him."

Abu Jahl was arranging his lines for assault, when he was spotted by Hadhrat Abdur Rahman bin Auf (radiyallahu anhu). The boys were on foot, while Abu Jahl was on horseback. One of the boys hit a leg of the horse and the other that of Abu Jahl. This caused both to fall down and Abu Jahl was unable to get up. The boys left him in this condition. Mu'awwaz bin Afra (radiyallahu anhu), brother of Hadhrat Mu'aaz bin Afra (radiyallahu anhu), then went and further wounded him with his sword, so that he might not drag himself to his camp. Finally, Hadhrat Abdullah bin Mas'ood (radiyallahu anhu) attacked him and cut-off his head from the body.

Hadhrat Mu'aaz bin Amr bin Jamooh (radiyallahu anhu) says: "When I hit Abu Jahl with my sword, his son Ikramah was with him. He attacked me on my shoulder and cut my arm, leaving it hanging by the skin only. I threw the broken arm over my shoulder and kept fighting with one hand. But when I found it too awkward, I separated it from my body by placing it under my foot and pulling myself up and threw it away."

Questions

1. What is the ruling of physical fitness/training in Islam?

2. What is the shar'ee view regarding spectating of sports?

3. Mention five sports that we are encouraged to participate in?

Chapter 4 – Bad Habits

MUSIC

1. Rasulullah ﷺ has said: "Music generates hypocrisy in the heart just as water causes crops to grow."(Mishkaat)
2. Rasulullah ﷺ was ordered to destroy all musical instruments. (Abu Dawood)
3. Once we become used to listening to music, we forget our Deeni obligations and we become lethargic, and evil then sets in.
4. Some of the present-day Arabic, English or Urdu Nazms with music and tunes resembling Hindi and English songs are also in the category of music as they resemble and mimic songs and are accompanied by music.

EFFECTS AND PUNISHMENT FOR LISTENING TO MUSIC

1. On the Day of Qiyaamah, molten lead will be poured into the ears of the listeners of illicit songs and music. (Ibn Asaakir)
2. Listening to music is a useless activity that wastes our time and takes us away from the remembrance of Allah Ta'ala.
3. Music has an effect on one's thoughts and behaviour. A simple example of this is that, one often sees people swaying their bodies or tapping their feet when listening to music.
4. Many songs convey wrong messages and tempts people to engage in drugs and illicit relations.

5. The ideas that are presented in music go against the teaching of the Qur-aan and Shariah and influences one to rebel against Deen.
6. Hadhrat Abu Hurairah (radiyallahu anhu) has narrated that Nabi ﷺ said "Listening to music is a sin and to sit in the gatherings of music is disobedience and to take enjoyment from it is kufr." (Nailul Autaar)
7. The listener of music is deprived of the enjoyment of Ibaadat. He doesn't feel like reading the Qur-aan. Salaah becomes a burden to him. His contentment is shattered; he will want to listen to more and more of the latest music. Eventually due to the hypocrisy, he feels irritated with the Azaan, Deen and the people of Deen until he develops a dislike for them and avoids them. He has now reached the border of Islam and Kufr! May Allah Ta'ala protect us! Aameen.
8. Hadhrat Abu Hurayrah (radiyallahu anhu) has narrated that Rasulullah ﷺ said, "Close to Qiyaamah, the forms of some people of my Ummah will be transformed and changed into that of monkeys and swines." The Sahaabah (radiyallahu anhum) asked, "O Rasulullah ﷺ, will these people be Muslims?" Nabi ﷺ said, "Yes, they will testify that there is none worthy of worship but Allah and that I am Allah's messenger and they will also fast." The Sahaabah (radiyallahu anhum) asked, "O Rasulullah ﷺ! Then why will this happen to them?" Nabi ﷺ said, "These people will become accustomed to musical instruments and singing girls and they will drink wine. One night, they will be involved in drinking wine and in futilities and amusements. In the morning, their features will be transformed." (Singing & music by Mft A.Rauf quoting ibne hibbaan)

Chapter 4

REWARDS OF NOT LISTENING TO MUSIC

Rasulullah ﷺ said: "On the Day of Qiyaamah Allah Ta'ala will say, 'Where are those people who, in the world, protected their ears from listening to satanic music and their eyes from looking at singers? Separate them from the people.' The angels will separate them from the people and seat them on mounds of musk and amber. Thereafter, Allah Ta'ala will command the angels, 'Let them hear my pure and majestic hymns.' The angels will then recite to them from the zikr of Allah Ta'ala in such a beautiful and melodious voice which they never heard before." (Jam'ul Fawaaid)

NB. The one who acquires the passion of listening to the Qur-aan will never get enjoyment in listening to anything else.

SMOKING

WHAT DOES ISLAM SAY ABOUT SMOKING

1. Allah Ta'ala states: "And do not throw yourself into destruction with your own hands." (S:2, V:195)
2. It is not permissible for a Muslim to indulge in anything which is a hazard or danger to his health or life.
3. Smoking in Islam is considered MAKROOH (Allah Ta'ala and Nabi ﷺ dislike it). It has a bad smell which chases away the Malaaikah.

4. Smoking destroys the good (health, wealth, time, etc.) that Allah Ta'ala has given us and we are warned in the Qur-aan not to bring destruction upon ourselves with our own hands.

WHAT DOES A CIGARETTE CONSIST OF?

1. CARBON MONOXIDE: This prevents oxygen from reaching the brain and heart and other muscles.
2. POISONOUS LEAD: This accumulates in the body and the body fails to break it up.
3. NICOTINE: A poisonous substance which, if injected into the arteries, can kill a person. Nicotine raises the blood pressure, increases the heart rate and contracts blood vessels near the skin.
4. TAR: This makes the teeth yellow, causes tooth decay and inflammation of the gums.

WHAT ARE THE PHYSICAL HARMS OF SMOKING?

1. Smoking affects one's health severely. It prevents oxygen from getting to the skin, which is why smokers appear to be pale and unhealthy. It also aggravates psoriasis (a skin problem).
2. Smokers always suffer with bad breath.
3. Smoking affects ones physical performance. It causes shortness of breath whereby you will find that smokers cannot perform as well as non-smokers.
4. Smokers generally heal much slower. This is because smoking affects the body's ability to produce its natural manner of healing.
5. Studies show that smokers get more colds, flu, bronchitis and pneumonia than non-smokers.

6. Teenagers that smoke generally damage their growth because their bodies lack the nutrients to grow and to fight illnesses properly.
7. Smoking also can cause fertility problems in both men and women.

SMOKING AFFECTS THOSE AROUND US

By smoking, one affects those around him. The families and children of smokers can end up with all kinds of breathing problems. Infants exposed to smoking are extremely vulnerable to asthma, bronchitis, ear infections and sudden infant death syndrome.

FINANCIAL EFFECTS OF SMOKING

All wealth, sustenance, etc. that comes to us is actually given to us as a trust from Allah Ta'ala and we will be questioned about it on the day of Qiyaamah. Allah Ta'ala says in the Qur-aan, **"Do not squander your wealth. Indeed the squanderers are the brothers of shaytaan, and shaytaan was ungrateful to his Rabb."** (fifteenth juz)

1. We have to use our wealth in accordance to the laws of Shariah. Burning our money on cigarettes is not permissible.
2. Consider a person who smokes one packet of cigarettes a day for 30 years. How will he justify this waste of money to Allah Ta'ala?
3. This money could be used for the poor and contributing towards the upliftment of Muslims in all facets of life and would be more than enough to go for Haj and Umrah many times.

HOW TO GIVE UP THIS HABIT?

Ask ourselves, "Why are we smoking in the first place?" Generally the answer is: STRESS. Will smoking solve our problems? Certainly not! We have created a mind-set for ourselves based on the society we live in. We feel that when we have stress, the immediate solution is to smoke. This is the same reasoning drug addicts and alcoholics use; that this habit will solve their problems. With this mind-set, a person will never give up any bad habit. The mind is saying that it is a bad habit but the sub-conscious mind regards it as a solution for our problems.

1. The first step is to convince ourselves that this habit is certainly not a solution to any problem; rather it is a separate problem on its own.
2. Be strong and control your will power.
3. The solution for all our problems is 2 rakaats of Salaah. All the pious people of the past and present solved their problems through Salaah. All conditions are in the control of Allah Ta'ala. We have to ask Him only. Every difficulty comes to us from Allah Ta'ala because of our actions. When we know that the solution is only in Allah Ta'ala's hands, how can anyone besides Allah Ta'ala solve our problem!!!
4. Join the company of the pious. Refer to a righteous, pious Aalim for further advice.

Chapter 4

INTOXICANTS

In the light of the Qur-aan and Hadith anything that makes one drunk and affects one's ability to think clearly is evil and forbidden. This includes alcohol and all forms of drugs.

Rasulullah ﷺ has warned us of the curse of Allah Ta'ala on the person who takes alcohol, buys it, sells it, transports it, offers it to others or drinks it. All of those involved falls under this curse.

WHY DO PEOPLE TAKE INTOXICANTS?

1. One of the main reasons is BAD COMPANY. Accompanying "friends" that indulge in taking intoxicants.
2. PEER PRESSURE: The social environment (our friends) makes us feel that without taking intoxicants we are not a man, etc."
3. EXPERIMENTING: Seeing it on T.V., etc. or hearing about the "enjoyments" of using it.
4. DEPRESSION: One can't cope with reality so he wishes to "run away" from his problems. He wants to just feel happy again and have fun, etc.
5. GAINING ENERGY: To take such substances for studying, dancing, fighting, sports, etc.

HARMS OF INTOXICANTS

1. The Qur-aan and Hadith declare all kinds of intoxicants to be **HARAAM** and a Major sin.
2. One's ibaadaat become void of reward for forty days.

NB: If someone is intoxicated, it still becomes compulsory to fast in Ramadhaan and read the five daily Salaah whether one gets reward for it or not. If one wasn't sober and the time of Salaah had passed by, then it will be compulsory to make Qadhaa.

3. Things one will never do in normal circumstances are done when intoxicated. There is an incident of a person who was threatened with his life if he didn't do one of 3 crimes: to kill someone, to commit zina (adultery) or to drink wine. He chose the intoxicant (wine) and ended up doing the other two crimes as well due to not being in his senses.

4. The one who takes intoxicants is apparently fearless and daring. In actual fact, he is paranoid. He always feels that people are after him. He gets frightened when alone. He always wants to be in dark areas and hang outs. He suffers with low esteem and an inferiority complex. He has mood swings. He feels threatened and therefore acts aggressively at times. He is never composed in behaviour. He is either too "high or too low" but never balanced. This is his first AZAAB (punishment) in this very world i.e. everything will disturb/upset him. May Allah Ta'ala save us. Aameen.

5. Many people are hooked for life after the first "Pull." After being addicted, no matter how many times they may try to reform, they tend to relapse. Therefore, never go near taking intoxicants otherwise one will be "CURSED" for life. This is a reality - with the exception of those few whom Allah Ta'ala has mercy upon. If we are involved, never lose hope in the mercy of Allah Ta'ala.

6. These drugs affect our body, mind, family, financial wellbeing and the whole society.

Chapter 4

7. One will suffer from insanity, stomach disorders, ailments of the intestines, loss of appetite, etc.
8. One can become financially ruined, causing one to then resort to stealing and begging in order to satisfy one's desires.
9. One develops the habit of speaking lies, becomes irresponsible, shameless and oppressive.

HOW DOES A PERSON GIVE UP THIS HABIT

1. One should ask himself, "Why am I taking intoxicants?"
   Is it peer pressure? If it is, then he should change his circle of friends.
   Is it to try and escape from a problem? If so, then one must understand that one is not alone. Turn one's attention to Allah Ta'ala and know that HE is with one at all times. Speak to a responsible adult who will help to analyse and solve the problem.
2. Always remember, "WE CAN DECIDE WITHIN OURSELVES HOW THIS IS GOING TO AFFECT US."
3. THINK, CONTEMPLATE, PONDER, AND REFLECT.
4. Think about the less fortunate and what difficult conditions they have to live in. Thank Allah Ta'ala for what He has blessed you with.
5. Take up the **courage** and **will power** and then adopt practical solutions.
6. Get help. Don't be in **denial**. Most drug addicts believed that they had **control** over themselves until it was too late.

GAMBLING

The Qur-aan states, "They ask you about wine and gambling, say in both these are great sins."

THE STATUS OF GAMBLING AND ITS HARMS

1. In the light of the Qur-aan and Hadith, gambling is Haraam and a major sin.
2. Gambling is addictive. The gambler is cursed and deprived of blessings in everything.
3. Consuming the food, etc. purchased from the income of gambling will result in haraam and evil actions. Therefore many addicted gamblers get involved in zina, swearing, fighting, killing, theft, drugs etc.
4. The addicted gambler becomes deprived of halaal livelihood.
5. It is a cause of hatred, animosity, aggression and quarrels.
6. It affects one's family and social circles.

WHAT IS REGARDED AS GAMBLING

Any game that a person plays where he has to pay a fee to enter and stands a chance of winning some money or reward, e.g.:

1. Taking part in crossword puzzles where participants are charged a fee.
2. Commercial lotteries (lotto).
3. Playing cards and betting one's wealth and property.
4. Chess, backgammon, etc.
5. Cell-phone competitions where a fee is charged.
6. Playing the machines in casinos.

Chapter 4

7. Betting on horse racing.
8. Betting on sports events.

NB: A Muslim should not even visit a casino even if he is not gambling or playing any of the machines. These are places that are cursed by Allah Ta'ala.

PHYSICAL HARMS OF GAMBLING

A gambler suffers from many harms and sicknesses. He is always under severe stress, suffers from high blood pressure, headaches, insomnia, etc. Many gamblers eventually end up committing suicide.

HOW DOES ONE GIVE UP THIS HABIT?

1. Firstly, make sincere Taubah and Istighfaar. Beg Allah Ta'ala to forgive you and help you to leave this evil sin.
2. Ensure that one's earnings are Halaal and not even a cent is doubtful. Consult a pious Aalim for advice.
3. Change your company. Don't be around friends who gamble. Look out for good friends who will take you towards good rather than towards evil.

Questions:

1. What is the meaning of hypocrisy? _____

2. Hadith: Listening to singing and music is a _____ and sitting by it is _____ and to derive pleasure from it is an act of _____ .

3. Are nazams or anasheed with music permissible?

4. Mention two punishments on the day of Qiyaamah for those who listen to music?

5. Mention the Hadith in which Nabi ﷺ tells Hadhrat Huzaifa (radiyallahu anhu) that people's faces will be changed into that of monkeys and swines.

6. What is the reward for those who stay away from music in this world?

Chapter 4

7. Mention four reasons as to why people start taking intoxicants?

8. If a person takes intoxicants, then for how many days is his ibaadat void of reward?

9. If a person takes intoxicants, does that mean he must not attend the masjid daily for Salaah and he should not fast in Ramadhaan?

10. Mention few tips on how a person can stop this habit of taking intoxicants.

11. How would you explain to a friend of what Islam says about smoking?

12. Mention some physical harms of smoking?

13. What is the solution for PROBLEMS Muslims face after knowing well that smoking only aggravates it?

14. What is the status of gambling in Islam?

15. Explain some examples of gambling?

16. How should a person give up this evil habit?

Part 2

In this section ......

- Evil glances, Photography, Television, Cell Phones
- Pornography, Masturbation, Zina, Dating, Suicide
- Conduct and Duties at Home,
- Mashwara, Employment
- 7 Habits of Highly Successful Muslim youth
- Conclusion

Chapter 5

Harms of Casting Lustful Glances[1]

By: Hadhrat Moulana Hakeem Muhammad Akhtar Saheb (rahmatullahi alayh)

In this time and age, due to the shamelessness and immodesty, which has spread through pornography, television, videos, internet, cell phones, cinema, novels, etc., many people's lives have been destroyed. Young people have ruined their youth in zina (fornication) and masturbation. Marriages have been broken due to unlawful love affairs. On a social level, society is plagued with problems such as rape, prostitution, child molestation, homosexuality, AIDS, etc.

The question arises as to what is the root of all these problems. May Allah Ta'ala reward our Mashaa'ikh and pious predecessors, who look at the world with the eyes of the heart, enlightened by the light of the Qur-aan, Hadith and the burning love of Allah Ta'ala. They have diagnosed all these sicknesses to be brought about by one deadly disease. The root of all these problems is the **SIN OF THE EYES, CASTING LUSTFUL GLANCES** at women. Unfortunately today, people do not even consider casting evil glances to be a sin, when actually it is the root of innumerable vice and sin.

Another reality which people are totally unaware of is that by protecting one's eyes from lustful glances, one is promised the taste of the sweetness

---

[1] This is a summary of the original article

of Imaan. Once the sweetness of Imaan enters the heart, it will never be taken back. Thus by protecting the eyes, one is given glad tidings of a good death.

Rasulullah ﷺ said: "Verily the evil glance is a poisonous arrow from the arrows of Iblees. He who abstains from casting evil glances, I will grant him such Imaan, that he will feel the sweetness of it in his heart."

(Kanzul-Ummaal; Vol. 5, pg. 228)

Harm No. 1: Disobedience of Allah

Casting evil glances is clearly forbidden in the Qur-aan. Allah Ta'ala says: "O Nabi, tell the believing men to lower their gazes." (Surah Nur; Aayah 30, Juz 18) Do not look at ghair-mahram women[2] (strange women) and handsome boys. Therefore, he who casts evil glances is opposing the clear and explicit command of Qur-aan, and one who opposes the clear and explicit command of Qur-aan is guilty of committing a **HARAAM** act.

Harm No. 2: Breach of Trust

The one who casts evil glances is breaching the trust of Allah Ta'ala.

It is mentioned in the Qur-aan that Allah Ta'ala knows the mistrust of the eyes and that which the hearts conceal. (Surah Mu'min; Aayat 18; Juz 24)

Allah Ta'ala uses the word mistrust. This indicates that we are not the owners of our eyes rather we have been entrusted with them. This is the reason why suicide is forbidden, because we are not owners of our bodies. Allah Ta'ala has entrusted us with our bodies. Since they are a trust from

---

[2] Note: It is permissible for one to look at a mahram female, e.g. one's wife, mother, grandmother, sister, daughter, granddaughter, fathers and mothers sisters and grandfathers' and grandmothers' sisters, one's nieces.

Allah Ta'ala, it is forbidden to use it against His pleasure, to harm or to put an end to it. If we were owners of our bodies then perhaps we would have the right to use them the way we desire. To misuse this trust of Allah Ta'ala is a great crime. The one who casts evil glances is breaking and misusing the trust of sight which Allah Ta'ala has granted him. The breacher of this trust cannot become the friend of Allah Ta'ala. How beautifully a poet has said:

> The "thief of sight" can never have the crown of "friendship" which Allah placed upon his head.

Harm No. 3: Curses of Nabi ﷺ

The one who casts evil glances is cursed by Nabi ﷺ.

It is mentioned in a Hadith "May the curse of Allah be upon the one who casts evil glances and upon the one who presents him/herself to be looked at." (Mishkaat; Pg. 270)

If casting evil glances was a minor sin, then Nabi ﷺ, being a mercy to mankind would not have cursed the offender. The curse of Nabi ﷺ is clear proof that this is a very severe crime. The meaning of curse is to become distant from the mercy of Allah.

This is why after the command of guarding the eyes. Allah Ta'ala mentions "Guard the private parts." Through the blessings of guarding one's eyes, his private parts will also be safeguarded. On the contrary, if a person cannot guard his eyes, he cannot guard his private parts.

Harm No 4: An Action of Stupidity

Hadhrat Hakeemul Ummat Moulana Ashraf Ali Thanwi (rahmatullahi alayhi) said: "Every sin is a sign of stupidity and foolishness. For a person to commit a sin is already an indication of the deficiency in his intellect. He is disobeying such a Being in whose hands is our life and death, our health and sickness, peace and comfort. If his intellect was sound he would never commit sin. As for the one who casts evil glances, Hadhrat says that he is extremely foolish. By casting glances, he attains nothing other than restlessness in his heart.

Harm No. 5: Pain to the Heart

The heart experiences great amount of grief and sorrow when looking at pretty faces. When a person casts evil glances at any beautiful girl then one comes to know of her shape and features. "Her eyes are like this, her nose is like that and she has a model's face..." This causes restlessness and uneasiness in the heart. By casting evil glances and making oneself go through regret and grief, the anger and wrath of Allah Ta'ala descends. As a result of this, the heart becomes restless and uneasy. One does not have a moment of contentment in the heart and life also becomes bitter.

Harm No. 6: Weakness of the Heart

By casting evil glances, the thought of that beautiful girl continuously comes into the heart and mind. Through this, the heart becomes weak and sickly. In the commentary of the verse: *"Indeed Allah is fully aware of what they do,"* Ruhul Ma'ani explains the following:

1. Allah is aware of how you turn your eyes around to cast evil glances.

2. Allah is fully aware of the movements of all the limbs. Allah is watching how he uses his hands, legs and other limbs in order to obtain his beloved. Whereas the perpetrator is totally unaware that Allah Ta'ala is watching his every move.

3. Allah Ta'ala is fully aware of his final aim and that is zina and fornication:

"I AM FULLY AWARE OF YOUR EVERY MOVE. IF YOU DO NOT ABSTAIN, THEN THERE WILL BE SEVERE PUNISHMENT!"

Thus, in this verse there is an indication that he will be punished if he does not repent. Casting evil glances is the first stage towards zina and fornication, through which a person becomes shameless and then humiliates and degrades himself in both worlds. This is why Allah Ta'ala forbade the very beginning stage of casting evil glances. The example of this sin is like an escalator which automatically takes a person to the final stage, as soon as he puts his foot on the first step. That action whose beginning is evil, what can be expected of the end result?

Harm No. 7: Premature Ejaculation

By casting evil glances the sexual desires increase due to which the heat and temperature of the body rises. This in turn, makes the semen thin and watery by which a person gets the sickness of premature ejaculation. Such a person is unable to fulfil the rights of his wife due to which their marital relations and eventually their family life is destroyed.

Harm No. 8: Ungrateful towards one's wife

Casting evil glances brings about ingratitude within the heart. When a person is looking at so many faces and features then his own wife does not remain attractive to him anymore. Hence, he becomes ungrateful thinking to himself that he did not get a good-looking wife. And if she is good-looking, then he thinks to himself that she could have been more beautiful. In this way, he becomes ungrateful of Allah's favours. As for the one who guards his eyes out of Allah's fear, and does not look at other women, then even if his wife is not so beautiful, she will always be attractive to him and in this manner he will always remain grateful to Allah Ta'ala for His favours.

Chapter 5

Harm No. 9: Weakness of eyesight

By casting evil glances, a person's eyesight becomes weak. This is because by guarding one's gaze, one is grateful to Allah for the blessing of sight and the reward of gratefulness is increase in blessings as mentioned in the Qur-aan Shareef:

"If you are grateful then We will most definitely increase you in blessings."

Casting evil glances on the other hand is ingratitude and the punishment of ingratitude is severe, as is mentioned in the Qur-aan Shareef.

"And if you are ungrateful then know that My punishment is severe."

Harm No. 10: Sexual Desires are aroused which eventually lead to zina and masturbation

By casting evil glances, the sexual desires are inflamed and aroused within a person. This is such an evil act that does not leave you until it takes you to the final stage of sin wherein a person does not even see beauty anymore. Guarding one's private parts after casting evil gazes becomes impossible. This is why after the command of lowering the gazes Allah Ta'ala reveals "guard the private parts". From this we see that by protecting the gaze the private parts also become protected, and if the gaze is not guarded then the private parts also does not remain secure from sin.

The Cure for Casting Evil Glances

By: Hazrat Moulana Shah Abrarul-Haq Saheb (Rahmatullahi alayh)

Hadhrat Moulana Shah Abrarul-Haq Saheb *(rahmatullahi alayh)* has formulated some very important guidelines for protecting the gaze. Read them once daily with the intention of self-reformation.

The harms of evil glances are so numerous that sometimes one's Deen and worldly life are both destroyed. The evil effects of this spiritual disease is spreading rapidly nowadays. Accordingly, it seems appropriate to mention the cure and remedy to all the harms which have been mentioned.

One can protect one's gaze by adhering to the following practices:

1. When women are passing by, keep the gaze low no matter how much one has an urge to look. If your gaze accidentally falls on her, immediately lower it no matter how difficult it is, even if there is fear of losing your life.
2. Perform a minimum of two Rakaats Salaah for every evil glance and also give some money in charity according to your means.
3. Repent excessively.
4. Completely abstain from intermingling with females who are not your mahram.
5. Do not read love poems or novels. Abstain completely from movies, television, videos, magazines, unnecessary "surfing" on the Internet and all kinds of pornography.
6. Stay away from the environment of nudity and disobedience.
7. Do not adopt the company of those who are involved in the disobedience of Allah Ta'ala.
8. Ponder over the fact that Allah Ta'ala is watching you all the time. The Malaaikah (angels) are with you recording your evil deeds in a book that will be presented before Allah. The ground on which you are walking on will bear witness to your evil actions. Your limbs with which you commit these sins will also bear testimony against you. Think about Whose commands you are breaking.

Chapter 5

By practicing the above mentioned guidelines, *Insha Allah*, your evil desires will come under control. Gradually you will be cured of the love of everything besides Allah Ta'ala. Eventually your heart and soul will perceive such rewards that will bring ecstasy to your soul all the time. The heart will experience such tranquillity that even the kings do not dream of. It will seem as if a life of hell has been changed into a life of heaven.

Hadhrat Abu Hurayrah *(radiyallahu anhu)* narrates that Rasulullah ﷺ said:

"Every eye will weep on the Day of Qiyaamah except for the eye which was lowered from unlawful glances and that eye which stayed awake in the path of Allah and that eye which shed tears in the fear of Allah (even if a tear be as small as the head of a fly)." (Tafseer Ibn Kaseer: Surah Nur, Aayah 30)

PHOTOGRAPHY, VIDEOS, TELEVISION, CELL PHONES, D.V.D, YOU TUBE, ETC

HARMS:

1. Hadith: "Indeed on the day of Qiyaamah, the most tormenting punishment will be given to those who make (animated) pictures." (Bukhaari)
2. The viewer of T.V. etc. listens to music, watches dancing and nudity, looks at women, listens to bad and vulgar language and watches violence all the time. All the above are separate Major sins combined in the T.V, D.V.D etc. So the viewer gets

the combined sin and is therefore cursed, grows in hypocrisy and will be severely punished on the day of Qiyaamah.
3. The T.V, D.V.D, etc. are addictive and its evil effect is long lasting. Even after giving them up, it will take years before one's mind and heart are cleansed of its evil influence.
4. Like drugs, the viewer of T.V, etc. thinks his sin to be trivial and feels that he has control. Only when he is determined to give it up does he realise how much of control it had over him.

SOLUTION:
1. Get rid of the T.V, D.V.D.s, camera, etc. Don't sell it. Destroy it.
2. Make sincere Taubah and Istighfaar.
3. Increase in one's ibaadat: Salaah, Qur-aan, zikr, etc.
4. At other times, keep oneself busy in some other permissible activity (e.g. reading Islamic books and articles, gardening, physical activity, etc.).
5. Join the company of the pious.

PORNOGRAPHY

Pornography is the watching of filthy films, photographs, etc. which display pictures of nude men and women. When a person doesn't have any hayaa in him, it leads him to evil acts like pornography.

Chapter 5

What is Hayaa?

Hayaa (shame and modesty) is one of the most valuable qualities a Muslim. Any person who does not have hayaa (shame) is disliked by Allah Ta'ala, Nabi (sallallahu alayhi wasallam), the Malaa'ikah, the pious and people in general. Muslims must always be full of shame and modesty. Shamelessness, immorality and rude behaviour destroy our Imaan and lead us to shameless sins.

Our noble Ulama have explained that Hayaa is a natural quality *(fitrat)* that Allah Ta'ala has created within us that stops us from committing shameless sins. When one is about to commit a sin, a feeling from inside stops one from going forward and doing that sinful act. We should look after and take care of this hayaa as it is a great gift of Allah Ta'ala and will stop us from committing many other sins.

Harms of pornography

Only one who has no hayaa will engage in the despicable sin of pornography. May Allah Ta'ala save us, our children and the entire Ummah of Rasulullah ﷺ from this evil sin. According to many doctors, pornography is an addiction worse than many drugs.

1. It is proven that a person who watches porn damages his human relationships and leads him to becoming abusive towards his wife.
2. The pornographic images stay in the mind for the rest of the viewer's life. This is why many psychologists believe pornography to be the cause of many psychological problems.
3. The effect that pornography has on the brain is very similar to that of street drugs.
4. Watching pornography at a young age causes one to engage in HARAAM sexual activities at a young age. Performing sexual

activities at younger ages in turn creates many other problems. Teenage pregnancies and sexually transmitted diseases have increased because of people watching porn.
5. Teenagers engage in dangerous sexual activities from these films, and this has led to serious health issues such as throat, tongue, and mouth cancer.
6. Almost two thirds of divorce cases are linked to pornography. Those who view pornography want to act out what they view and if they are not satisfied, then this results in divorce.
7. While a person may first watch pornography out of curiosity, it soon grows into a habit and then goes totally out of control.

PRACTICAL STEPS TO OVERCOME PORNOGRAPHY

1. Firstly, make sincere taubah and beg Allah Ta'ala to forgive you.
2. Keep on making dua and ask Allah Ta'ala to help you to leave this evil sin.
3. Understand the harms of this sin and make a firm resolve to leave it out forever.
4. Keep yourself occupied with other permissible activities. Staying occupied and not remaining idle lessens the chance of negative thoughts entering one's mind.
5. Keep company with good friends, because being around the right group of people, including family and friends, is a great support for you.
6. Seek help from someone senior you trust and respect.
7. Place Islamic reminders such as printed Qur-aanic verses or Ahaadeeth in rooms where your computer or phone is kept, to remind you of the consequences of viewing such videos.

Chapter 5

8. Fasting is something highly recommended in the Hadith. Fasting curbs an individual's sexual urges. Therefore, a person should try and keep lots of optional fasts.
9. Perform Salaah at its prescribed time, and regularly perform Tahajjud Salaah (night Salaah).
10. After Fajr, recite Aayatul-Kursi and the three Quls, three times (daily).
11. Developing Taqwa (fear of Allah Ta'ala) is of the utmost importance. Taqwa enables one to be aware of one's actions and to refrain from sinful behaviour.
12. Place computers in areas where they are clearly visible within the house. Don't use Internet browsers that have private browsing modes.
13. Install website filters on computers that block out inappropriate websites.
14. Spend time in Jamaat and in the company of pious Ulama.

ADVICE FROM AN EX ADDICT (is it appropriate???)

I am a 25 year old male, recovering from addiction to porn and masturbation.

It all started at about the age of eleven, when I accidentally discovered masturbation. Back then I did not understand what I was doing and did not realise that this was haraam (but I have to say that, even though I was young I had a feeling that this was wrong). Anyway I continued in this fashion for a year or two, and then I discovered porn. At first I was too embarrassed to simply walk into a shop and buy a magazine, so I would literally look in people's garbage, in the hope of finding pornographic material. I remember staying awake late at night and turning on the TV once my parents slept, in order to watch late night TV which often showed porn. (I remember in shame the lengths I would go to conceal my secret, e.g. closing the door, but not completely so that I can hear approaching footsteps and hiding a pornographic video underneath a loose floorboard that was nearly discovered by my father).

It got worse, and I felt very guilty. Then one day, I was about 13 years old when I took a brave step and confessed to my father, who was extremely supportive and gave me practical tips to my problem. It worked for a few months and my father thought he was successful, but unfortunately I relapsed and went back to my old ways.

I continued like this for a few years until about the age of fifteen/sixteen (throughout this time I always felt guilty and ashamed but continued anyway), that was when the internet became main-stream. To me this was the start of a new level in watching porn, as it made it so easy, (no need for embarrassing walks in to an adult shop, and of course the ease of access and variety of porno content on the web). I started off by simply watching nude pics and downloading free video-clips (you see the porn barons are very much like drug dealers, you get your first joint for free, then you're hooked and forced to go back to the dealer, but this time you have to pay to get the harder content). However, after about 2 years the free stuff simply was not enough; I needed more to quench my ever-increasing lustfulness. This was when I crossed another fence, using my credit card. This continued until about the age of twenty. This was when it really got out of control as I started to contemplate visiting prostitutes; you see watching porn alone was not enough. Again, it's like drugs, you start with basic drugs and end up with the worst. Again the internet made it very easy to do this, as prostitutes advertise themselves on the web on certain specialist websites. At first, like the previous post I would only call these women, it kind of gave me a kick. I would justify it to myself by saying that, 'it's not haraam to talk, as long as I don't actually act on my feelings', but yes... you guessed it, I moved on to the next level and committed Zina.

Chapter 5

After the first experience which left me feeling very guilty, I decided to repent to Allah Ta'ala and stop watching porn, but once you have been addicted to something for so long it's very easy to relapse. In fact, I started to visit prostitutes on a regular basis.

After a year or two, I decided that the only way to solve my problem was to get married. Unfortunately, marriage only helped for a few months, and then I relapsed once more.

However, things changed exactly one year ago. As I'm sure you have realised, this beast of an addiction has been the story of my life, it has absolutely consumed me in every way, I have tried so many times to slay the beast, but every time I fail. Yet, something happened to me exactly one year ago that allows me to stand before this forum today, and announce that I have finally slayed this beast. In fact, today is my first year of victory. Like all other addicts, whenever I repented, I knew at the back of my mind that this will not last. One year ago, when I repented, I came to the realisation that I cannot have this thought at the back of my mind, as it made my repentance worthless. I then sat down and brainstormed all the evil consequences of porn; I came up with the following,

1. The most important one of course is going to JAHANNAM.
2. Constantly feeling guilty and worthless.
3. Constantly feeling ashamed of myself, this led to poor self-esteem and lack of confidence.
4. Wasting my precious time. Time that can be spent learning new things or simply enjoying the company of my family.
5. Having to constantly lie to cover my tracks, and then to lie again to cover my previous lies, and so on.
6. Sexual contact with my wife became a chore rather than something to look forward to, as I simply was no longer excited by my wife.

7. The feeling of utter emptiness after masturbating compared to the feeling of joy when hugging my wife.
8. The amount of money wasted: I can honestly say that in the space of about ten years, I blew approximately fifteen thousand pounds (R250 000) on porn and prostitutes. This money could have gone to the poor, it could have gone towards my house, it would have paid for about ten holidays, or at least four/five visits to the holy city of Makkah Mukarramah.
9. The inability to do anything that would please Allah Ta'ala (such as read Qur-aan, or help a Muslim), as I always felt "what's the point of doing a good deed, as I have committed so many disgusting sins."
10. The utter humiliation I would feel had my wife found out, not to mention the enormous amount of pain I would cause her had she found out I was watching porn and even cheated on her'.

So, how did I stop? It's a combination of everything really.

1. Constantly reminding myself of the ten disadvantages outlined above (I have them stored on my organiser, and read them every day).
2. Reading Qur-aan, making dua every day and giving charity.
3. Never staying home alone if possible.
4. Performing my Salaah on time.
5. Going to my wife whenever I felt the desire.
6. Remembering how guilty, depressed and ashamed you feel after committing the sin of watching porn or masturbating.
7. A lot of you will probably agree with me that you watch porn when you are bored and have free time on hand. There is a

Chapter 5

verse in the Qur-aan about free time and how it should be used. I also recently heard a lecture in which the Imaam said that all evil comes from spare time, as this is when a human is at his most vulnerable, you have nothing to do, nothing to pre-occupy your mind, so in order to fill this void, you commit a sin such as watching porn. The message here is always occupy your mind with something useful (read a book, visit relatives, play with your children, start a project or do anything as long as it is not haraam). Never remain idle when you have time on your hands as boredom can be your downfall, and lead you to the wrong path.

Apart from these seven points, I have a few more tips that have worked for me.

1. One year ago, I took an oath to Allah Ta'ala that if I was to relapse I would fast for 120 days continuously.
2. Every day, I go in front of the mirror and I psyche myself up, screaming 'NEVER', 'NEVER', 'NEVER', over and over again, ('NEVER', as in, I will 'never' go back to my old ways again).
3. I have a secret book that I purchased specifically for this purpose. I have marked all the dates of the year on it for the next couple of years. Next to every day I either have a tick which would represent a successful day, in other words a day I did not watch porn in, or I would have a cross, which would represent failure. Alhamdulillah I now have 365 ticks, and not a single cross. I look at all these ticks every day, and it gives me a sense of achievement. I would not want to see a cross in this book, as it would symbolise a return to the old ways. Seeing that cross would seriously depress me, hence I avoid it at all cost.

I hope these tips will help. Please make dua for me as I want to continue on the right track. I know I can. I know I can. I know I can. Allah is on my side. Allah is on my side. Allah is on my side.

MASTURBATION

Masturbation has become one of the most common sins youth are engaged in. The evil effects of bad company and watching of pornography leads one to this despicable sin of masturbation. Many youngsters are involved in the sin of misusing their hands. This is a major sin in the sight of Allah Ta'ala and brings about darkness in one's heart. The Qur-aan states: "Those whose desires exceed the limits are transgressors." Allah Ta'ala has given us legal and permitted ways of satisfaction and this is through Nikah. Satisfying oneself in a prohibited way is breaking the commands of Allah Ta'ala.

WARNING

Allamah Aalusi (rahimahullah) has written in his tafseer: Those who commit zina with their hands are accursed. Allah Ta'ala will punish the nation whose people use their private parts in unlawful ways. On the Day of Qiyaamah, this nation will come forth with their hands pregnant. (They will be those who used to masturbate).

There are seven types of people that Allah Ta'ala will neither look upon with mercy, nor purify or raise them with the Ulama, but will rather gather them with those who will be entered into Jahannam. If only they would repent, for Allah Ta'ala is merciful to those who repent.

Chapter 5

1. The one who masturbates.
2. The doer of an evil act of sodomy.
3. The willing recipient of the evil act of sodomy
4. The drunkard.
5. One who physically abuses his parents.
6. One who mistreats his neighbours so badly that they curse him.
7. One who commits zina with his neighbours wife or female neighbour.

HARMS OF MASTURBATION

The greatest harm of masturbation is that one gets the curse of Allah Ta'ala. The Ulama have mentioned many other harms, some of which are mentioned below:

1. One's memory is weakened.
2. One becomes physically weak.
3. The digestive system is harmed.
4. Impotency and premature ejaculation is a direct result of masturbation. This causes difficulties in married life later on.
5. One's mental health is also affected.
6. One's courage and determination diminishes.
7. One always prefers to be alone rather than mixing with others.
8. One becomes very lazy.
9. It leads to depression.

HOW CAN WE STOP THIS HABIT?

1. Stop watching porn.
2. Refrain from chatting with girls on cell phones, websites, chat rooms, pornography, indecent literature, etc. It may seem like

harmless fun until you are so caught up in it that there seems to be no escape.
3. Everything starts with a first step and we have to train ourselves to resist temptation.
4. Keep good company and good friends who would strengthen your Imaan and character.
5. Engage in physical activities. Don't laze around.
6. Above all, FEAR ALLAH TA'ALA! Think that Allah Ta'ala is watching, so many angels are watching and are present. One will have to stand before Allah Ta'ala whilst the entire creation witnesses one being taken to task for every evil act. How embarrassing it will be on that day!

ZINA / FORNICATION / ADULTERY

WHAT IS IT?

1. Zina is to have sexual relations with women other than one's wife.
2. Zina is such a serious crime that Nabi ﷺ rated it second to shirk.

CONSEQUENCES OF ZINA

- Allah Ta'ala becomes very angry.
- The reckoning in the hereafter will be very severe.
- The person will enter *Jahannam*.
- The *barakah* (blessing) of his *rizq* is lost.

Chapter 5

- He is deprived of doing good actions.
- He becomes hated and cursed in the eyes of the common people.
- The nation involved in *Zina* will be afflicted with droughts.
- The spreading of diseases and plagues.
- Earthquakes will occur frequently.
- The birth of illegitimate children.

Nabi ﷺ said: "Allah dresses whosoever He wishes with the dress of Imaan. Whenever someone commits zina, this dress of Imaan is taken away from him and not put back on until the person repents from this sin."

HOW DO WE REFRAIN FROM THIS ACT?

1. The Qur-aan states: "Do not come close to zina. Indeed it is utter shameless and a most evil way (S:17, V:32)
2. We are told not to even go near Zina. We should stay away from every avenue that will lead us to this terrible sin.
3. In the light of the Qur-aan and Ahaadith, all forms of communication with ghair mahrams (persons with whom nikaah is permissible) is haraam and a form of Zina. It comes in the Hadith that the zina of the eyes is in looking towards evil. This includes interacting via the cell phone or computer (e.g. internet, facebook, twitter, what's app, etc.)
4. Remember DEATH often.
5. Get married.
6. Join the company of the pious and spend time out in the path of Allah Ta'ala.

MARRIAGE

Nikaah is a great Sunnah of Rasulullah ﷺ. Allah Ta'ala creates lots of love between the husband and wife when they enter into the contract of nikaah. Nabi ﷺ has said that, one must not delay nikaah when the right match is found. Nikaah protects us from committing Haraam acts and keeps us pure and chaste.

To communicate with a strange girl via letters, sms, facebook, twitter, what's app, phone calls, etc. is impermissible. Allah Ta'ala says: "And you should not come close to adultery..." From this verse we understand that all things/ways that lead to adultery are also forbidden.

One should not communicate with ones future wife before getting married. This is not condoned in the Shariat and is not the way of our pious predecessors. Allah Ta'ala gave them barakah in their lives and their marriages were very successful.

Some parents allow their children to communicate with their fiancée before marriage under the pretext of "getting to know each other". This should not be allowed. Many a times the Nikaah is delayed due to the non-availability of a specific venue or not having a house or job. This may then lead a person to the evil sin of zina (adultery).

The solution is to make the Nikaah simple and get the Nikaah performed without any delay.

Chapter 5

SUICIDE

Our life in this world is a test. From time to time we do go through some difficulty and hardship. Allah Ta'ala will definitely test us. It is only in Jannah that one will experience happiness forever with no problems and difficulties. Whenever you are faced with a problem, remember to turn to Allah Ta'ala for help and assistance. Sabr (patience) will bring you great rewards.

Nowadays, people think that the solution to their problems lie in SUICIDE (killing themselves). The warning in the Hadith for suicide is very severe. Rasulullah ﷺ has said that any person who kills himself with a steel (weapon) would be an eternal dweller of Jahannam and he will have that weapon in his hand and will be thrusting it in his stomach for ever. He who drank poison and killed himself will sip that poison in the Fire of Jahannam where he is doomed for ever and he who killed himself by falling from (the top of) a mountain will constantly fall in the Fire of Hell and will live there for ever.

From this Hadith we learn that suicide is not the answer to our problems but rather it is only the beginning of all our problems. Don't become worried and distressed. Allah Ta'ala is always there for us. There is no problem that is so huge for which Allah Ta'ala cannot find a solution. Turn to Allah Ta'ala and you will find that Allah Ta'ala has all the solutions.

CAUSES:

1. DEPRESSION AND DISAPPOINTMENTS due to:
    a) Poor school or matric results.
    b) Girlfriend relationship broken up.

c) Things turned out contrary to one's expectation.
d) Divorce.
e) Loss of job, house, money, someone close, etc.
2. STRESS due to:
a) Too many responsibilities.
b) Black mailed or accused.
c) Frustration due to sickness, peer pressure, etc.
3. BAD COMPANY.
4. DRUGS AND INTOXICANTS.
5. MENTAL OR SPIRITUAL SICKNESS i.e. some are mentally deranged and others are under the influence of jinn, etc.
6. In short any failure in life, any disappointment or not being happy with Allah Ta'ala's decisions is what leads a person towards suicide.

SOLUTION:

1. Turn to Allah Ta'ala. All conditions come from Allah Ta'ala. Allah Ta'ala has the solution to all problems. Be convinced that ONLY Allah Ta'ala is in complete control. No one can comfort us like Allah Ta'ala. Trust Allah Ta'ala. There's definitely some good in every condition which one will realise in years to come.
2. Avoid actions that involve the disobedience of Allah Ta'ala like girl-friends, drugs, etc. which lead to sadness, depression, feeling void, hollow, empty, etc.
3. Adopt the correct means with all its requirements, then adopt tafweez i.e. leave the outcome and results for Allah Ta'ala to decide.
4. Join the company of the pious and totally avoid bad company.
5. Get help from the elders in your family or go for counselling to a pious Aalim in your area.

Chapter 5

QUESTIONS

1. List five harms of casting lustful glances?

2. How can one protect ones gaze?

3. How many major sins are committed by a person watching TV?

4. Who are those seven types of people that Allah Ta'ala will neither look upon with mercy, nor purify or raise with the scholars on the day of Qiyaamah?

5. What are the harms of masturbation?

6. Mention practical steps that will assist a person to overcome pornography?

7. What are the consequences of Zina?

8. How does one refrain from Zina?

9. Is communicating with strange females permissible, even if it is with a person's future wife?

Chapter 5

10. Mention five major causes of suicide? _____

11. What are the ways to get rid of the emptiness within that drags a person towards suicide? _____

Chapter 6

CONDUCT AT HOME

The beauty of Islam lies in our good social conduct to people around us. Before entering your home always make salaam loudly as this is a sunnah of our beloved Nabi ﷺ. The Qur-aan also teaches us to first seek permission before entering any private place. If no permission is granted to enter, one should not take offence but should leave nicely.

The conduct of our Nabi ﷺ inside his home was as excellent as it was outside. Hadhrat Aa'ishah (radiyallahu anha) has said that if Nabi ﷺ had to come out of his bed at night to go and perform Salaah then he would slowly remove the blanket, put on his shoes very quietly, open the door silently and go out. Then he would close the door silently.

We learn from this incident that Nabi ﷺ was careful not to cause any disturbance to anyone - even to his wives.

In our homes we should at least see to our own needs, for example: making our beds, clipping our nails, placing our clothes in the washing basket, arranging our clothes before going into the bathroom, neatening our cupboards, packing away our washing, polishing our shoes, etc. No person should be inconvenienced at any time because of us.

Chapter 6

DUTY AT HOME

Hadhrat Aswad (radiyallahu anhu) narrates that he asked Hadhrat Aa'ishah (radiyallahu anha), "What did Nabi ﷺ do at home?" She replied: "He would assist his wives in their housework."

Hadhrat Aa'ishah (radiyallahu anha) narrates: "Rasulullah ﷺ would mend his shoes, sew his clothing, and do the work that the ordinary people among you do." Nabi ﷺ used to milk the goats himself.

Nabi's ﷺ time at home was divided into three parts. One was for the ibaadat of Allah Ta'ala. One was reserved for himself. One was divided between serving others and himself. In this time he used to impart Deeni knowledge to the Sahaabah and they would also partake in meals with him. Nabi ﷺ would discuss incidents of the past with his family and also listen to their light hearted conversations.

At home we must get into the habit of reading the Fazaail-e-Aamaal and Fazaail-e-Sadaqaat. These two books are full of the advices of Rasulullah ﷺ. We will benefit greatly by reading and listening to these great advices.

MASHWARA (Consulting)

The Qur-aan Shareef lays great emphasis on making mashwara (consulting with our elders) in our day to day matters. Nabi ﷺ was also instructed to consult with the Sahaabah (radiyallahu anhum) regarding matters of importance. From this command we can understand the importance of making mashwarah. When we are young, we always want to do many things that come to our minds. Later on in life we regret over the mistakes and blunders we had done when we were young. The easiest way to overcome this problem is to consult with our parents, our Ulama and the wise people in our families. They will guide us to do that which is correct and right. If we don't consult, we will always end up in deep regret as mentioned in the Hadith of Rasulullah ﷺ.

ALWAYS HAVE A GOAL

The first goal of every human (Muslim or non-Muslim) is to recognise Allah Ta'ala. Once a person recognises Allah Ta'ala, he will worship, please, love and obey Allah Ta'ala. Muslims disobey Allah Ta'ala because of the weakness of their Imaan and not fully recognising Him.

Our objective and mission in life is to obey all the commandments of Allah Ta'ala as shown to us by Nabi ﷺ. If this is achieved, then we will be successful. However, if the material things of this world (e.g.

wealth, fame, etc.) were attained at the expense of any command of Allah Ta'ala or a single sunnah of Nabi ﷺ, we will not be successful and will accordingly have to face the consequences. After realising this, we should adopt a permissible trade or occupation with the intention of earning a Halaal income so that we can fulfil our necessities, assist the poor, etc. All this will be commendable.

NEVER BE IDLE

Always keep oneself busy in some work. Never be idle. An idle mind is a devils workshop. Keep yourself busy in the weekends and holidays. Have a list of chores to be done in one's spare time. This will help save time and prevent regrets. Nabi ﷺ discouraged laziness. Find work in your free time. In this way you will be able to earn some money as well as keep yourself occupied. A person who is occupied is safe from many sins.

Time is an Amaanat (trust) from Allah Ta'ala that is afforded to us. We will be questioned about the time we spent in this life. We will have to account for every second. Therefore, we should be wise about how we spend our time.

EMPLOYMENT

Nabi ﷺ said: Earning a Halaal livelihood is a Fardh duty after the (other) Faraaidh obligations.

Hadith: Wealth is an object of pleasure. Wealth acquired in a rightful way (in accordance with the Shariah) and spent in a rightful way will be of benefit to the owner.

Hadith: An honest truthful trader will be with the Ambiyaa, Siddiqeen and Shuhadaa on the day of Qiyaamah.

There is great virtue in working with one's hands. All Ambiyaa (alayhimus salaam), including our Nabi ﷺ, looked after sheep and goats or were occupied in some trade or business. Nabi ﷺ disapproved of begging and encouraged the Sahaabah (radiyallahu anhum) to occupy themselves in lawful occupation.

A pure and Halaal earning, no matter how inferior in the eyes of people, should be given preference over haraam earnings. Always be positive minded and confident and do not lose hope. A famous saying is: "Himmate Mardaa Madade Khudaa" - **"WHEN MAN TAKES COURAGE, HE GAINS THE HELP OF ALLAH TA'ALA."**

Chapter 6

7 HABITS OF A SUCCESSFUL MUSLIM YOUTH

Success in this world is directly related to the strength of our relationship with Allah Ta'ala. The further away one is from Allah Ta'ala and the teachings of Nabi Muhammad ﷺ, the less likely one is to achieve success in this world and, even less likely to achieve success in the hereafter. It is necessary for us to practice upon our Islamic teachings in order to become successful youth.

Below are seven qualities, derived from the Qur-aan and the teachings of Nabi Muhammad ﷺ, which will enable a Muslim youth to be highly successful.

1. BE TRUTHFUL

Being truthful is the greatest quality of a Muslim. Nabi ﷺ was known as As-Saadiq (The Truthful) even before his Nubuwwat was proclaimed. The highest position on the Day of Qiyaamah will be afforded to those who are TRUTHFUL. Many a times we feel it difficult to speak the truth especially when we make a mistake. We worry whether or not to disclose exactly what had happened. We are often afraid that if we speak the truth about what we have done or said, we will be in trouble with our parents or friends. What we forget is that Allah Ta'ala knows exactly what took place, whether the people around us know or not. A person experiences immediate mental and emotional relief when he speaks the truth even if he may be punished for what he did. Allah Ta'ala tells us in the Qur-aan, "This is a day in which the truthful will benefit from their truth. For them is Jannah, with rivers flowing beneath their eternal Home: Allah is well-pleased with them, and they with Allah. That is the great salvation, (the fulfilment of all desires)." (Al-Ma'idah 5:119)

One who speaks the truth is always respected by people whereas a liar is always disgraced in the sight of people. He will have to keep on lying to cover up for his original lie. Being truthful is not an option for Muslims; it is an obligation.

Rasulullah ﷺ has said, "Truthfulness leads to righteousness, and righteousness leads to Jannah. A man keeps on telling the truth until he becomes a truthful person. Falsehood leads to *Fujoor* (wickedness, evil-doing), and *Fujoor* leads to Jahannam. A man may keep on telling lies till he is recorded before Allah as a liar." (Sahih Bukhaari, Hadith #116)

Ultimate success is therefore achieved by living one's entire life as a truthful person.

2. BE TRUSTWORTHY

Are you considered a trustworthy person? Nabi Muhammad ﷺ was known in Makkah to be the most trustworthy person. If you want to progress in life you have to become trustworthy and reliable.

The Ambiyaa (Prophets) of Allah Ta'ala were all trustworthy people. Practice developing the habit of being trustworthy. When you accept a responsibility, ensure that you fulfil it. When others trust you, do not betray their trust.

You can read in the beautiful biography of our Nabi Muhammad ﷺ how people used to entrust him with their valuables, knowing that upon their return they would find their valuables safe and protected. His personal and business practices were of such a high standard that he was a perfect model for his community. Even before his Nubuwwat was proclaimed, he was known by all as the one who is most truthful and trustworthy.

3. HAVE TAQWA (Self-restraint and be Allah-conscious)

Perhaps the most difficult challenge while passing through youth is to restrain oneself from evil desires. Our success in life depends to a great extent on how well we are able to restrain ourselves from what is impermissible.

Shaytaan's goal is to make man a slave of his desires.

To become a highly successful Muslim youth, that is, a youth deserving of the greatest fortune, it is important that you develop Taqwa (self-restraint).

How wonderful it will be, if, in your old age, you can look back at your life and say to yourself, "All praise is due to Allah Ta'ala that I did not succumb to my desires and instead adopted Taqwa."

4. BE SYSTEMATIC AND ORGANISED

A Muslim youth must be systematic and organised in everything that he does. Never get into the habit of doing things haphazardly. If one is entrusted to do some work, make sure it is done correctly and efficiently. Rasulullah ﷺ liked people to be organised and systematic in what they did. He praised those Sahaabah (radiyallahu anhum) who were organised in their work.

5. BE FOCUSED

A Muslim youth must always be focused on what he is doing. He should never allow his mind to wander around and day dream. This takes his focus away from his goals.

Developing the habit of being focused ensures that one is awake, alert, and totally motivated to work on and complete the task at hand, whatever it may be. Video games and constantly changing scenes on television shows, makes one unable to concentrate and focus. Among the best ways of developing the ability to focus is to perform ones Salaah with deep concentration, focusing on the Greatness of Allah Ta'ala.

Do your best to develop the ability to focus, no matter what activity you are engaged in whether it is Ibaadat, in studies, at work or with family. Nowadays people have become so glued to their phones that they are completely oblivious of their surroundings.

6. BE PUNCTUAL

Punctuality is the stepping stone to success in any field. Successful people understand and appreciate the value of not only their time but the time of everyone else with whom they interact. Keeping people waiting for hours on end is neither something to be proud of nor a habit that has a place in the mind-set of a person who tries to be successful.

One of the central pillars of Islam is Salaah, and Allah Ta'ala and Nabi Muhammad ﷺ have given us clear reminders that we are to establish Salaah at their due times.

When 'Abdullah (radiyallahu anhu) asked, "Which deed is the dearest to Allah?" Nabi Muhammad ﷺ replied, "To offer the Salaah at its fixed time" (Sahih Bukhaari, Hadith #505).

If indeed your day is to be considered successful, you must have performed all the Salaah at their prescribed times. If your day is planned around the times of Salaah, you would perform Salaah at its time. This would also help in scheduling and completing other tasks punctually. By being punctual you demonstrate to others the tremendous value that Islam places on time — not only our time but that of everyone else with whom we interact.

7. BE CONSISTENT

Apart from all the habits listed above, the one that is sure to help you become a highly successful Muslim youth is that of being consistent. Be consistent on what you do. Don't be unreliable. Let your elders have trust in you, knowing full well that they can be assured that you will fulfil all the necessary tasks correctly and efficiently. Rasulullah ﷺ has said that the action that is most beloved to Allah Ta'ala is the one that is done with consistency, though it maybe a little.

We urge you to be as consistent as possible, especially in those areas of your life which are essential for your progress and success such as your Salaah, your fasting, your manners, your studying habits, etc.

O Youth.........
- Stay away from debt and borrowing money. Learn to live within your means.
- Don't violate the rights of others.
- Try and stay in the state of wudhu at all times.
- Try to secure a place for yourself under the shade of Allah's throne on the Day of Qiyaamah by staying in the obedience of Allah Ta'ala in your youth.
- Always think good, see good, hear good, have good aspirations, good intentions, good deeds, manners, habits, character and good friends.

Conclusion

Muslims always aspire to develop good habits because, in doing so, you draw nearer to Allah Ta'ala. If you really want to become a successful Muslim youth, then you should try your best to develop all the good habits a Muslim ought to have, and shun all evil and bad habits and ways.

We end of this book with a reminder to always strive to follow the life of our beloved Nabi Muhammad ﷺ. His message to the world is summarised in a Hadith of Hadhrat Abdullah ibn Abbaas (radiyallahu anhuma): "Abu Sufyaan (radiyallahu anhu) told me that Heraclius said to him, 'When I enquired of you what he (Muhammad ﷺ) ordered you, you replied that he ordered you to establish Salaah, to speak the truth, to be chaste, to keep promises, and to pay back trusts.' Then Heraclius added, 'These are really the qualities of a prophet.'" (Sahih Bukhaari, Hadith #846)

May Allah Ta'ala guide us all and keep us always in His obedience. Aameen.

Chapter 6

Questions

1. What is the meaning of "The beauty of Islam lies in our good social conduct?" _____

2. According to the life of Nabi ﷺ, what are also the duties of males at home? _____

3. A _____ and _____ are the two doors open for seeking guidance from Allah Ta'ala since the door of revelation is closed.

4. What is the daily objective and mission of every Muslim? _____

5. Explain… "Time is an amaanat". _____

6. Mention any hadith on earning halaal?

7. Explain in detail: "Is having a simple job better or begging?"

8. What is the meaning of "Himmate Mardaa Madade Khudaa"

9. What are the seven habits for every youth to be successful?

10. Explain what is TAQWA and to BE CONSISTENT in detail?

Chapter 6

Glossary of Terms

Shariah	Following the teachings of the Qur-aan and Rasulullah ﷺ
Buloogh	Puberty
Fardh	Compulsory
Satr	From the navel to below the knees (for men only)
Makrooh	Disliked action
Istibraa	Waiting till all the drops of urine have left the private path
Istinjaa	To clean the private path with water
Sunnah	The actions and speech of Nabi ﷺ
Janaabat	A state of impurity which makes Ghusal Fardh (compulsory) upon him.
Tawaaf	To go around the Ka'bah.
Zulfaa	To keep the hair up to the shoulder.

Waajib	Necessary
Amaamah	Turban
Itr	perfume
Ihraam	Wearing a two piece cloth before doing the rituals of Hajj or Umrah
Taqwa	Fear of Allah Ta'ala – self restraint
Fisq	Sinning
Azaab	Punishment
Zina	Fornication
Hayaa	Modesty

Notes

Please email your suggestions to info@talimiboardkzn.org

www.ingramcontent.com/pod-product-compliance
Lightning Source LLC
LaVergne TN
LVHW032006070526
838202LV00058B/6316